Bitch

Sweet TREATS

SWEAR WORD COLORING BOOK

I0439351

COLOR TEST PAGE

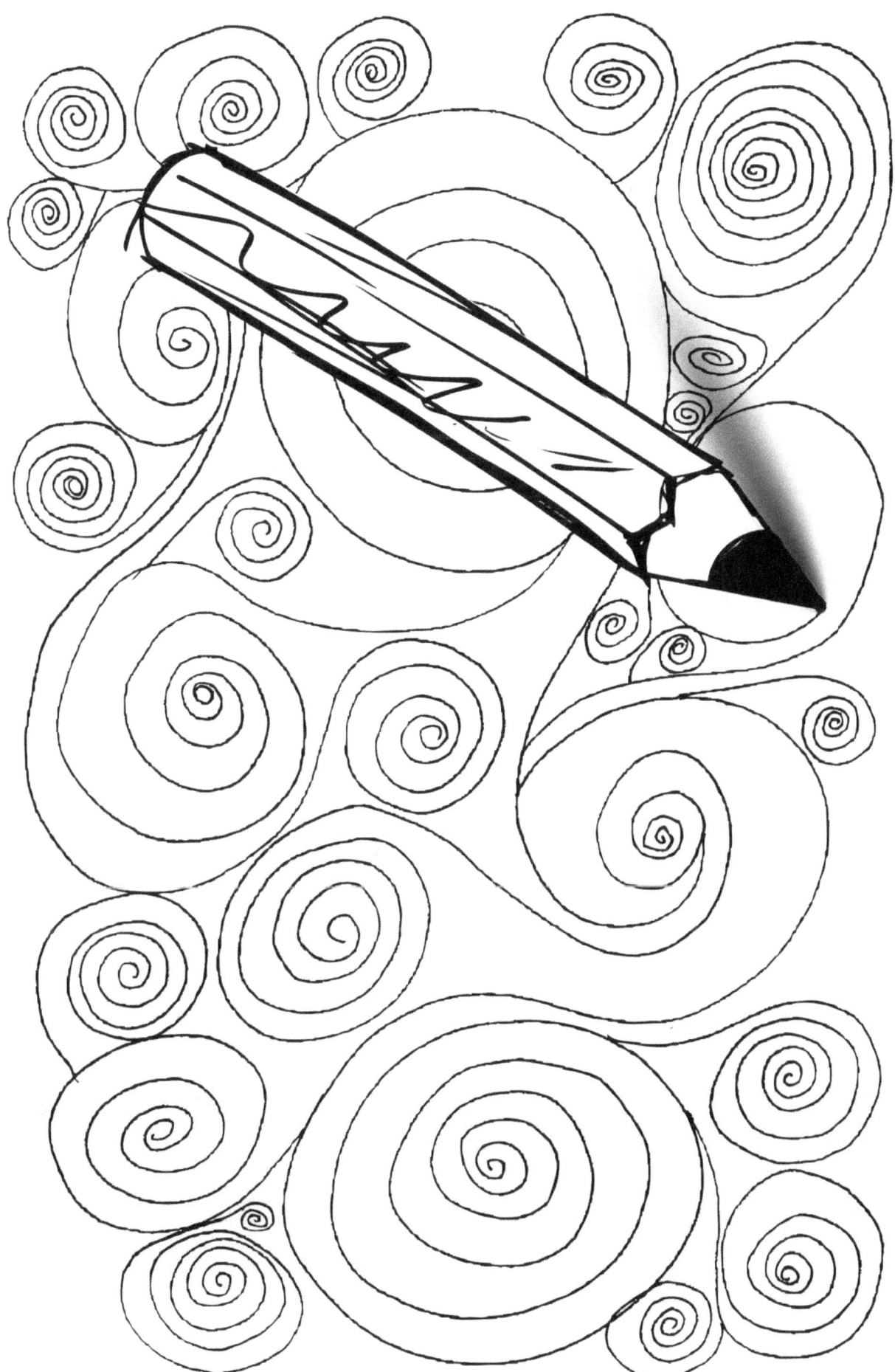

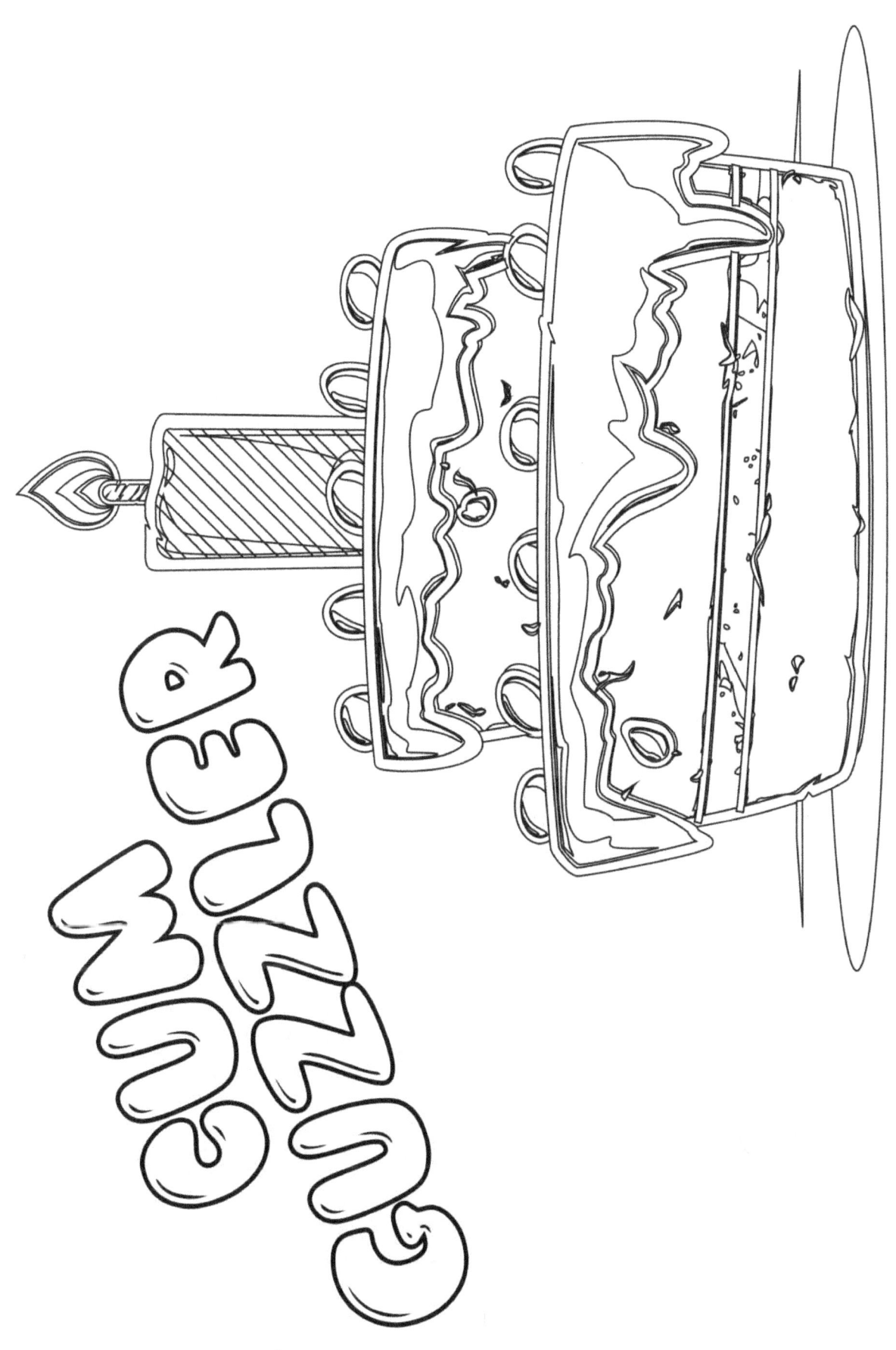

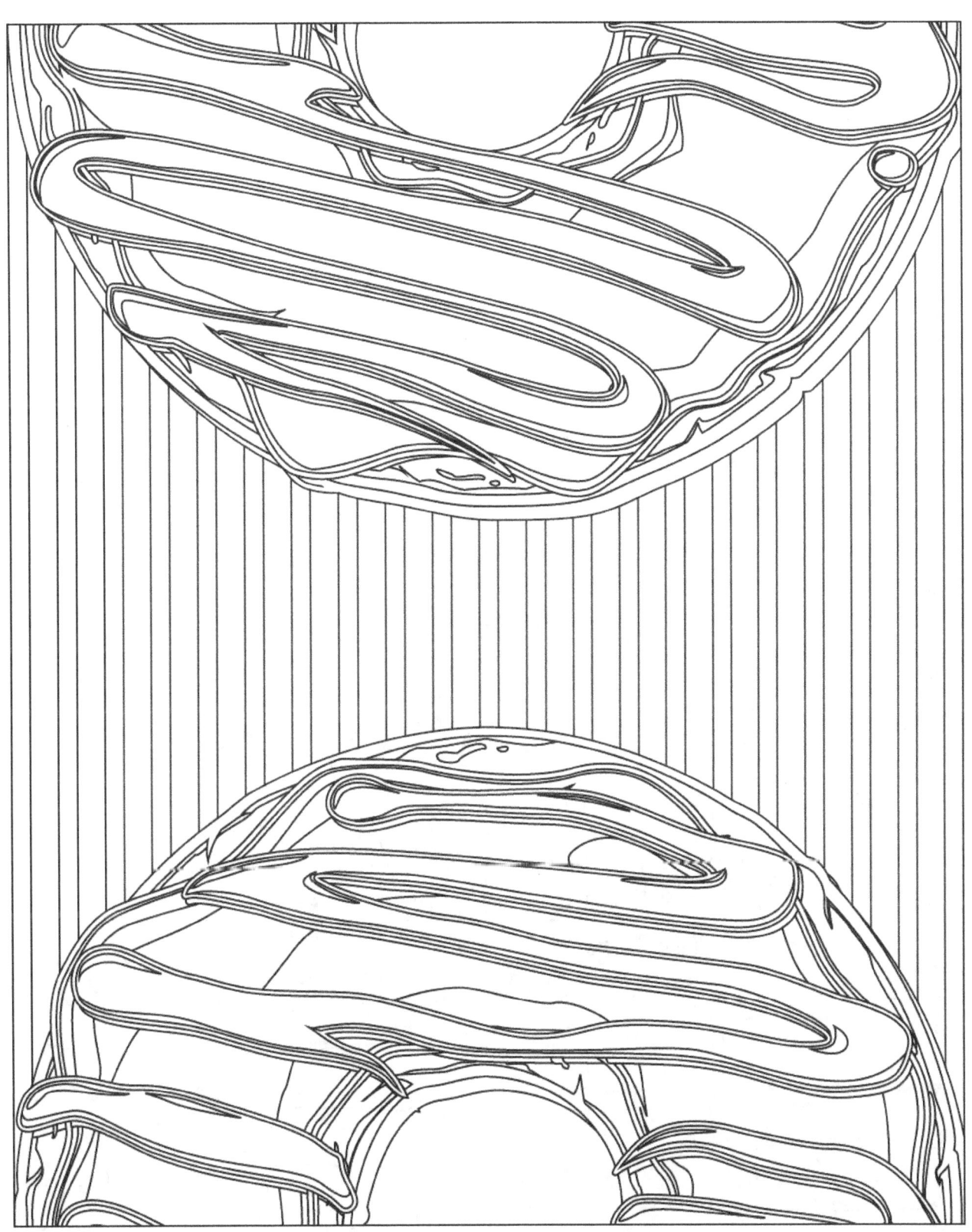

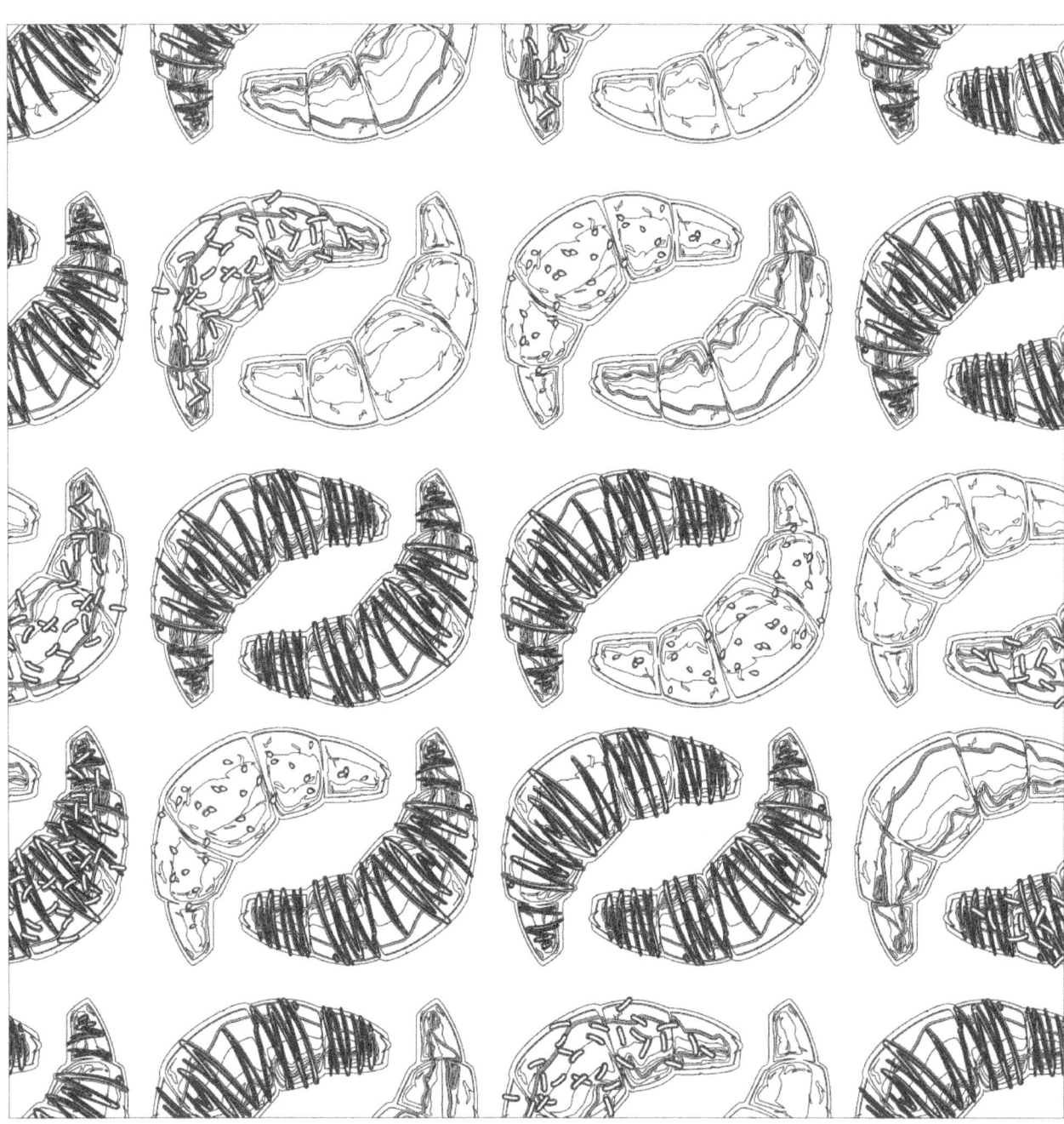

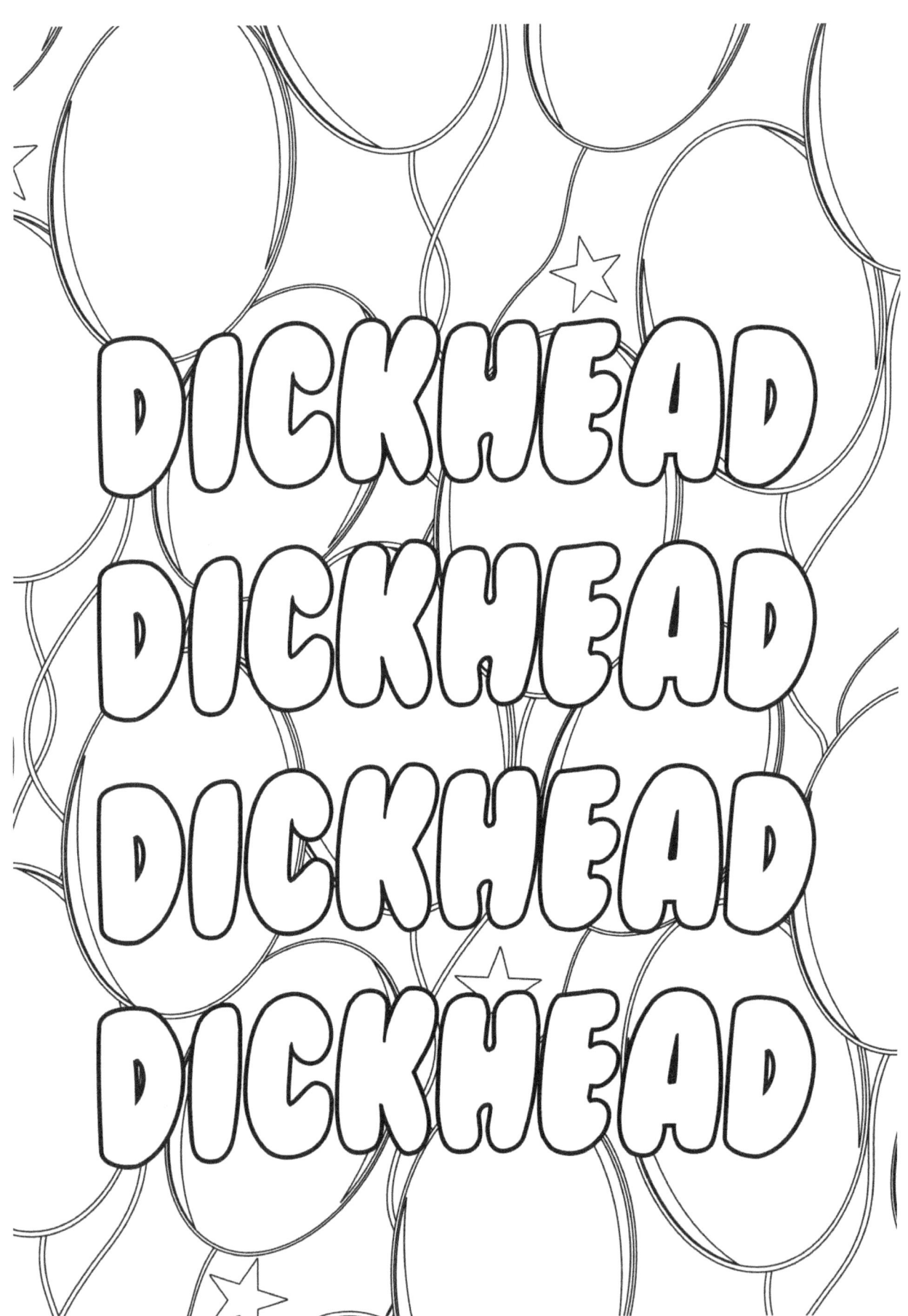

DICKHEAD

TEA

www.ingramcontent.com/pod-product-compliance
Lightning Source LLC
Chambersburg PA
CBHW081122280526
45787CB00007B/2937